INTRO2CRYPTO KID'S 1ST EDITION

By: Brian Scott

Dedication

This book is dedicated to my children and my grandson

Copyright © 2021 by Brian Scott

All rights reserved. No part of this book may be reproduced or used in any manner without the prior written permission of the copyright owner, except for the use of brief quotations in a book review.

To request permissions, contact the publisher at introtwocrypto@gmail.com

First paperback edition March 2021

ISBN 978-1-7369552-0-8 (paperback)

ISBN 978-1-7369552-1-5 (ebook)

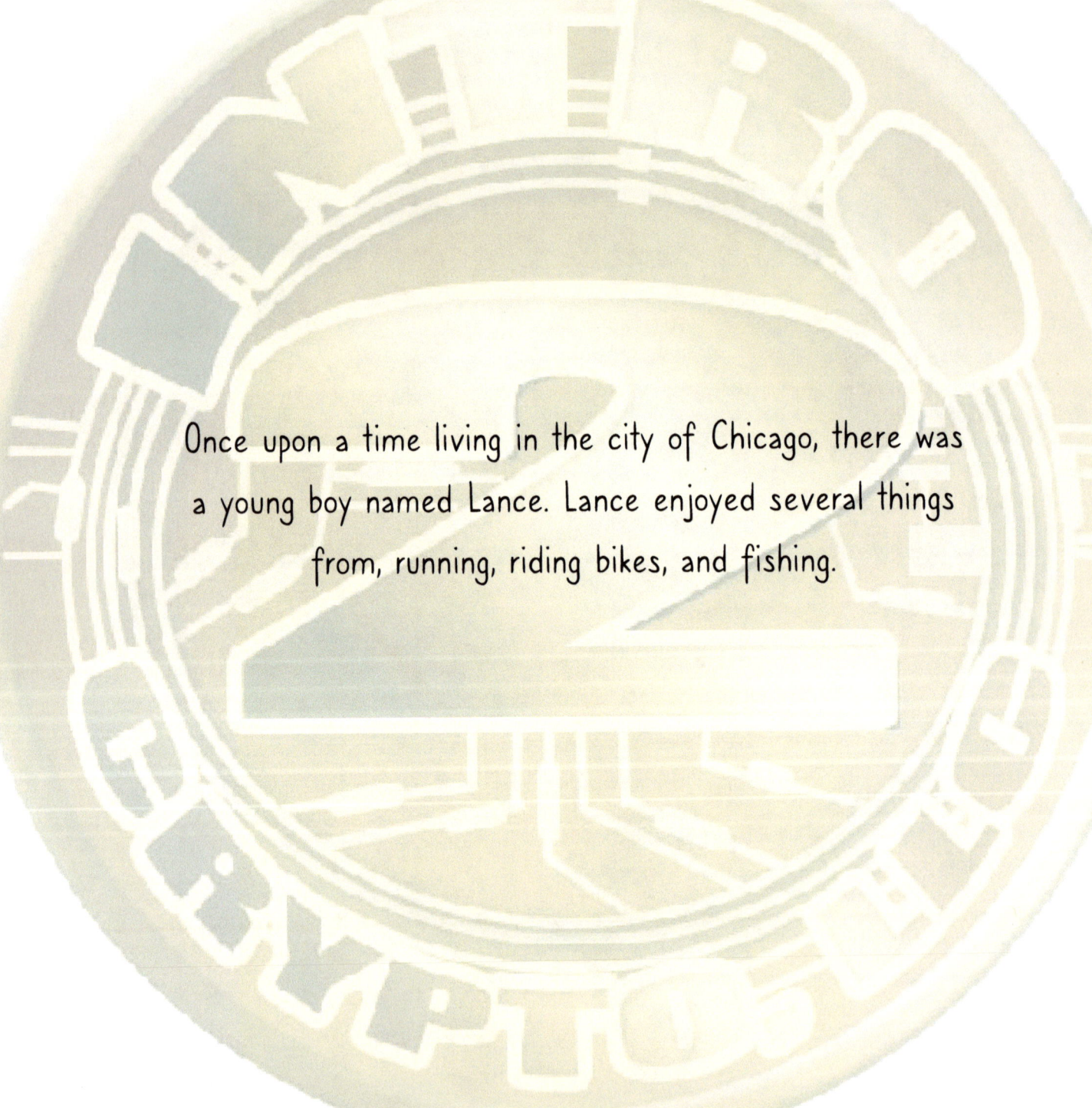

Once upon a time living in the city of Chicago, there was a young boy named Lance. Lance enjoyed several things from, running, riding bikes, and fishing.

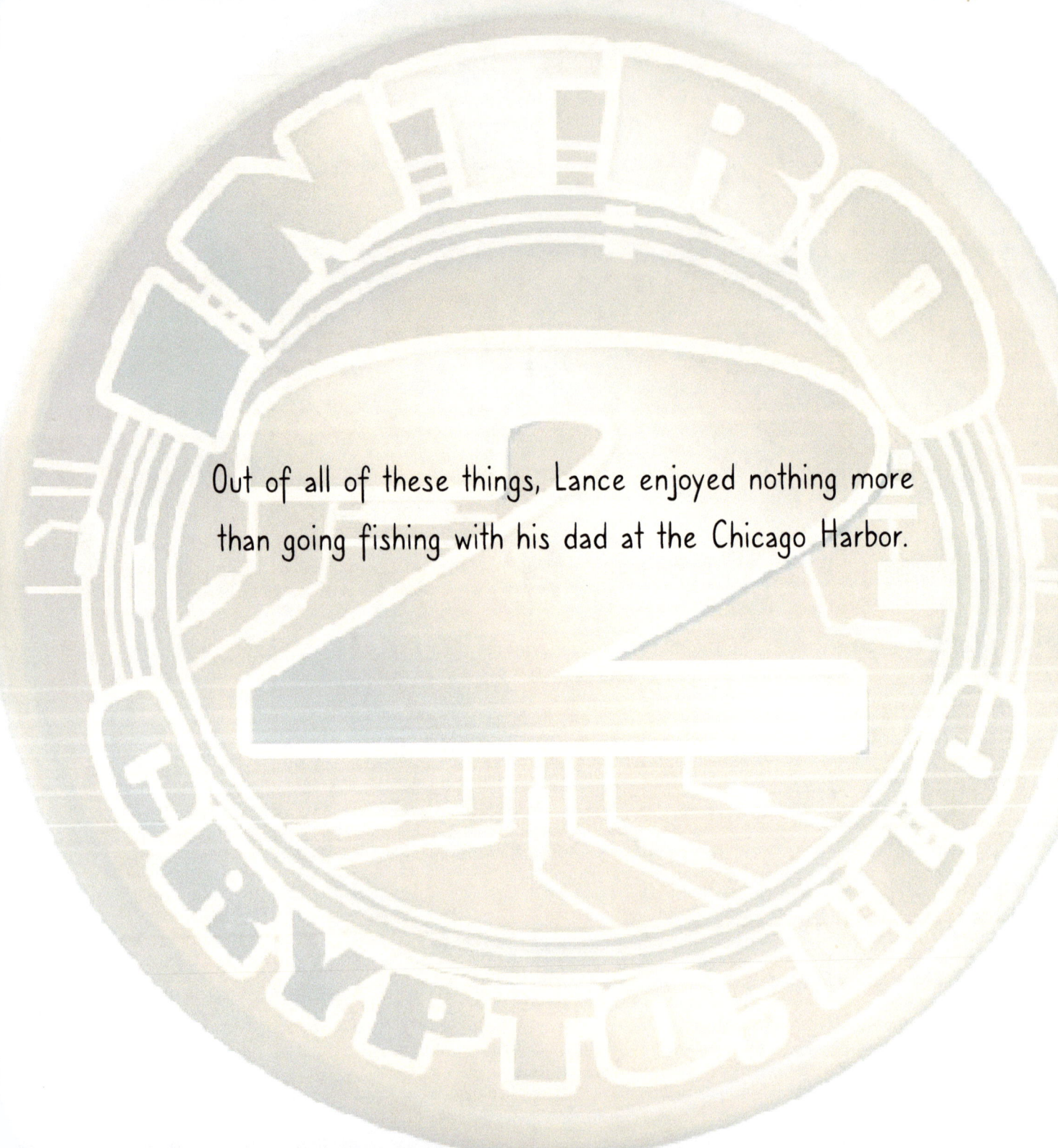

Out of all of these things, Lance enjoyed nothing more than going fishing with his dad at the Chicago Harbor.

One day while out fishing with his dad Lance caught a really big fish. It was by far the biggest fish he had ever caught. His dad said "Ok son, we can wrap it up. You have caught one of the biggest fish I have ever seen." Lance agreed he said "ok dad, can we take a picture with it?" his dad said "Sure"

After taking the picture Lance began packing up. Lance glanced over and saw this shiny object. It was something he had never seen before. Lance reached down and picked it up. He put it in his pocket and went on his way.

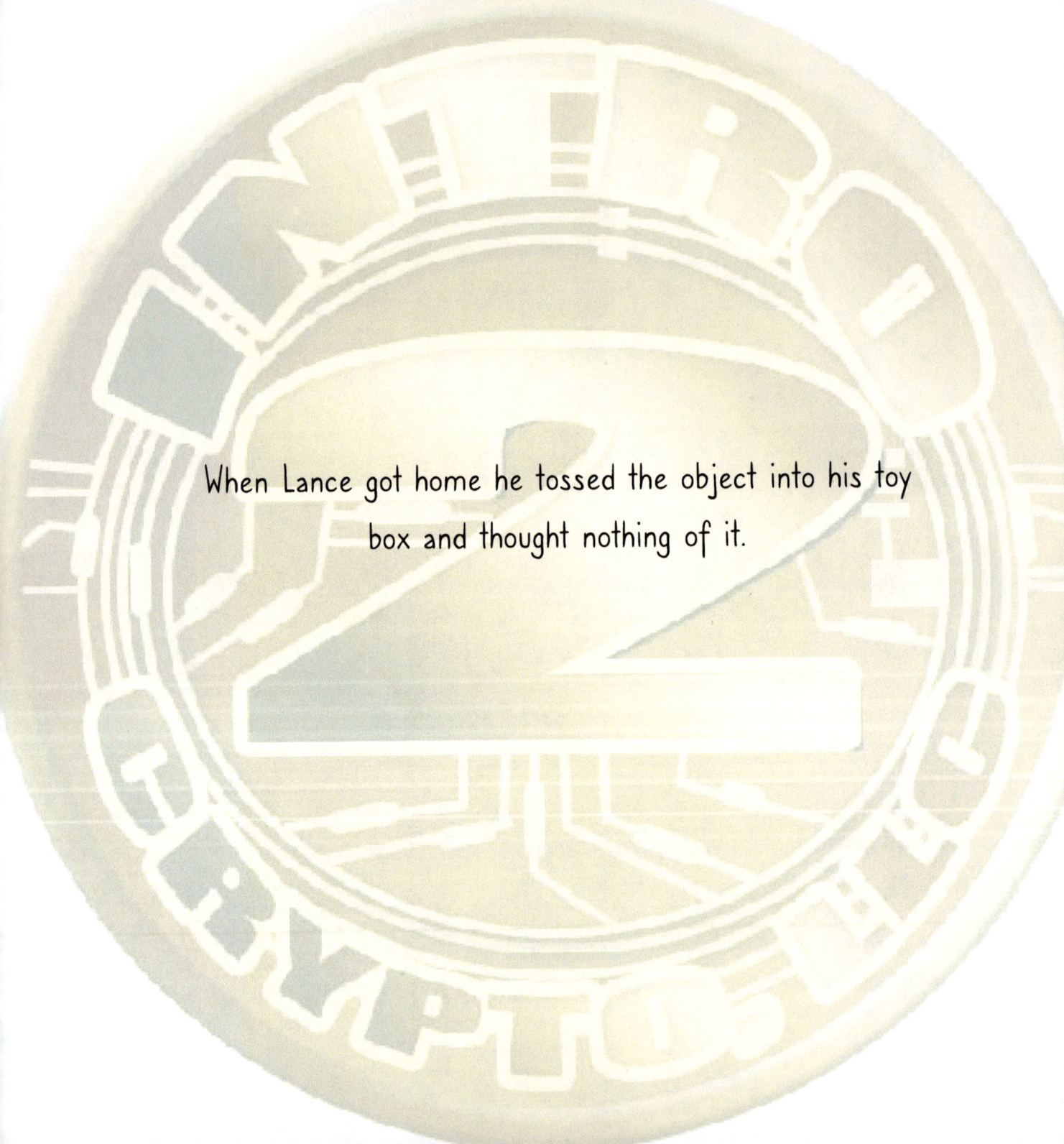

When Lance got home he tossed the object into his toy box and thought nothing of it.

One day while watching T.V. Lance saw a symbol that matched the symbol on the shiny object he found while fishing. It said, "Bitcoin the future currency if you want to be wealthy never give it up."
Lance began to think "I can be wealthy just from a coin? But how?"

Lance raced upstairs, opened his toy box and began throwing toys all over the room.
He finally found the coin buried underneath everything.

While holding the coin in his hand he began to look at the coin carefully.

Stamped on the back of the coin it read "Bitcoin be your own bank." Lance already knows what a bank does but he was very curious about what becoming your own bank really means.

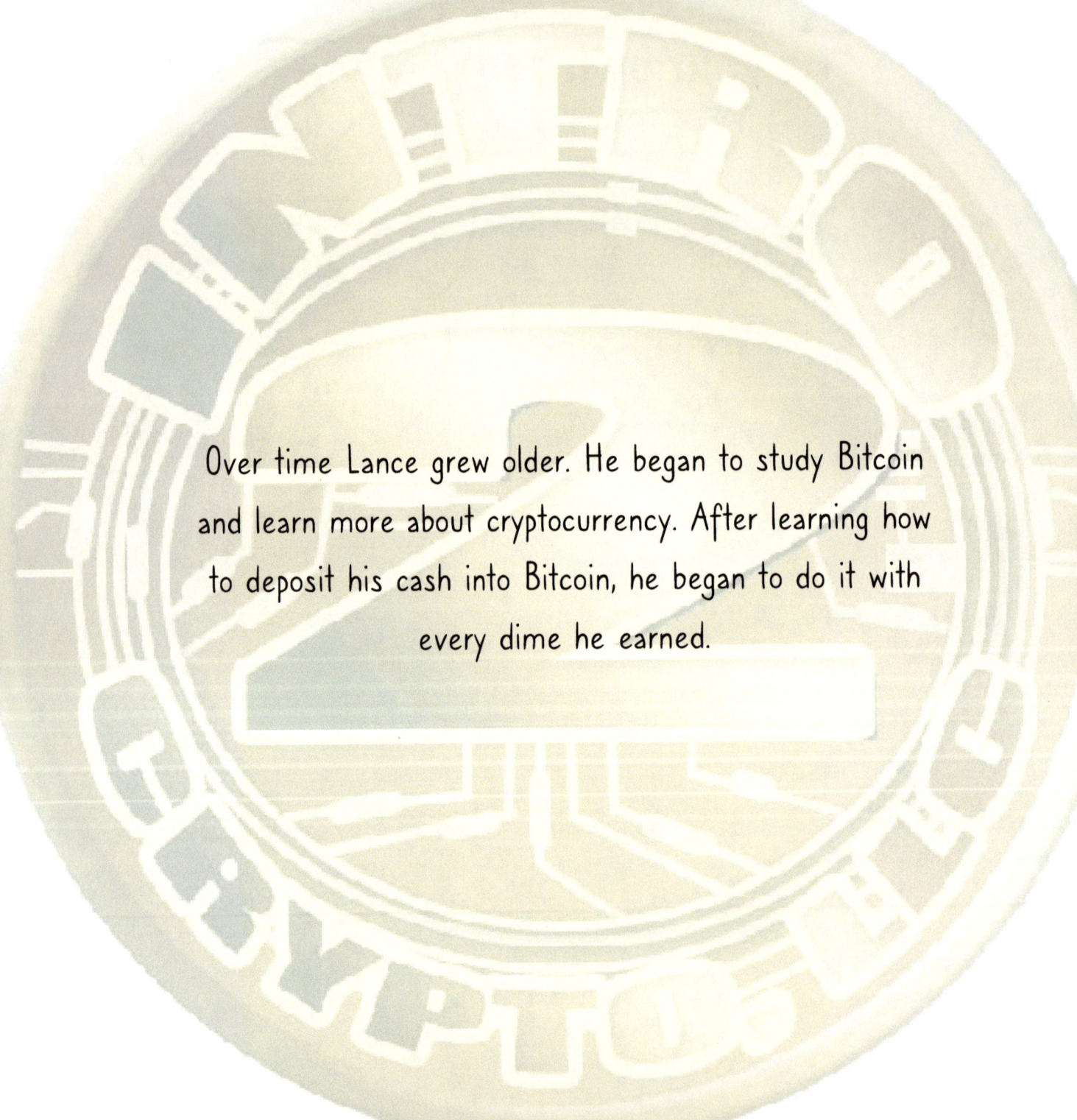

Over time Lance grew older. He began to study Bitcoin and learn more about cryptocurrency. After learning how to deposit his cash into Bitcoin, he began to do it with every dime he earned.

Lance would make money from mowing lawns, raking leaves, shoveling snow, and other odd errands. Every dime he would receive he would deposit it into Bitcoin.

Lance would always remember something his father always talked about. "Planting seeds and watching them grow." He never understood that until now. When Lance became older he wasn't depositing money into Bitcoin as much.

One day Lance was in dire need of money. He was fired from his job, his car had broken down and his rent was due. Lance was really in a bind. At the time it was a big buzz about Bitcoin on T.V. and all over social media.

Everyone was talking about how much Bitcoin had grown and if you were an early investor you are now seeing great benefits from buying Bitcoin. Lance always deposited money into Bitcoin and he knew he was one of those early investors. He just wasn't sure how much he actually had. So Lance decided to go check the balance of his Bitcoin account.

When lance checked his Bitcoin account he discovered it was $12,600,000 in U.S. dollars.

He realized through having the right mindset and having patience he was able to plant seeds for future generational wealth (Family). The 300 bitcoins he purchased at .75 cents each, had grown to $42,000 each over the years.

Now his financial problems were over, he jumped for joy screaming "I'm rich I'm rich, I'm freaking rich."

Lance was so thankful that he listened to that message on T.V. when he was a kid saying "If you hold on to this particular cryptocurrency it would be worth millions one day." It actually came true. He did not become wealthy overnight as he wanted but through the process of planting seeds like his father always taught him and being patient with the right mindset he was able to create generational wealth that will benefit his children and family forever. Now with this new wealth, he can go on to his next dream of opening his own business. To be continued!!!

www.ingramcontent.com/pod-product-compliance
Lightning Source LLC
Chambersburg PA
CBHW040029050426
42453CB00002B/51